■ □ ■ □ ■

CITY OF ASH

Writings from an Unbound Europe

■ □ ■ □ ■

EUGENIJUS ALIŠANKA

CITY OF ASH

Translated from the Lithuanian by
H. L. Hix and Eugenijus Ališanka

NORTHWESTERN UNIVERSITY PRESS

EVANSTON, ILLINOIS

Northwestern University Press
Evanston, Illinois 60208-4210

First published in Lithuanian as *Peleno Miestas.*

The author and translator are grateful to the following journals for previous publication of poems from this collection: *Iowa Review, 100 Words, The Review.* We also extend our thanks to Laima Sruoginis, editor of *Lithuania in Her Own Words: An Anthology of Contemporary Lithuanian Writing* (Vilnius: Tyto Alba, 1997), for including some of these poems.

Printed in the United States of America

ISBN 0-8101-1783-5 (CLOTH)
ISBN 0-8101-1784-3 (PAPER)

Library of Congress Cataloging-in-Publication Data

Ališanka, Eugenijus.
[Peleno miestas. English]
City of ash / Eugenijus Ališanka ; translated from the Lithuanian by Eugenijus Ališanka and H. L. Hix.
p. cm.
ISBN 0-8101-1783-5 (alk. paper) — ISBN 0-8101-1784-3 (pbk. : alk. paper)
I. Hix, H. L. II. Title.

PG8722.1.L53 P4513 2000
891'.9314—dc21

00-008902

The paper used in this publication meets the minimum requirements of the American National Standard for Information Sciences—Permanence of Paper for Printed Library Materials, ANSI Z39.48-1984.

▪ ▫ ▪ ▫ ▪

CONTENTS

▪ □ ▪ □ ▪

TRANSLATOR'S FOREWORD

EUGENIJUS ALIŠANKA'S TWO FAVORITE PUNCTUATION MARKS, the comma and the colon, are clues to his work, for as always in art the form is the vision. Commas signify both the separation and the linkage between elements in a series, and the elements of註išanka's poems are always serial. Having identified or imagined related elements, he leaves to the reader the tasks of coordination and subordination, just as one is left such tasks in ordering the elements in the series of experiences we call life:

> neither to leave nor to stay,
> no shore, this place has no beginning,
> the shorter the day, the clearer the man,
> neither absolved nor condemned, without the rust of frost,
> in the dark glade the gesture
> like lightning reveals rocks
>
> "solstice"

Stream of consciousness and surrealism also avoid enforcing an order of subordination, but Ališanka's poetry fits neither category. Stream of consciousness has, in spite of its name, no faith in the conscious mind but maintains instead a blind Freudian faith in the unconscious. It trusts what is presented to consciousness rather than what consciousness performs. Ališanka, in contrast, trusts the conscious mind, and in every series he sings, the elements are precisely chosen and perfectly imagined. Surrealism suffers from the fault Wallace Stevens identified: "It invents without discovering." But Committed Ališanka's inventions are also discoveries: the city of ash he invents holds all manner of revelations about the cities of brick and alabaster in which we live. His city holds

the last station, where shadows
roam the platforms, looking for their idea,
for their reflection, for their soul

"who will punish you when you return from the land"

Colons signify the presence of a relation, and in Ališanka's poems they have an almost mathematical sense: *a:b:c:d.* As in math, the relation is not specified, but it is announced:

but the flame grows clearer, and sands
like linden blossoms blast
exotic forms of hell: on the cape

of stone the runes of place-names glitter,
someone was here before spring died

"necklace"

These poems, then, are concatenations of non sequiturs, as are cities. Like cities, these poems add up to a logic of their own, and like cities these poems are where we live. Eugenijus Ališanka is the master of the run-on sentence, and the force that mastery gives these poems is their resonance with the run-on experience of our lives. His *City of Ash* paints an unforgettable picture of "the landscape of the soul."

CITY OF ASH

dogs' breath steams, cold air catches in your throat
when you step outside, glad to find
the familiar morning: bony earth,
skilled calligraphy of trees, even the smell,

this could be the landscape of the soul,
oikumene in november winds, something
more than the revelation of nonexistence,
incarnate in the rhetoric of nature, it could be,

every autumn I give you a frozen
cluster of ashberries: infertile years have taught me
to save, as if I could leave after death
preserved words, but every autumn

I recite an incantation to exorcise hunger,
every autumn I forget history,
why should you need it, when the sun rises
portending another short day

translated by Antanas Danielius and H. L. Hix

solstice

neither to leave nor to stay,
no shore, this place has no beginning,
the shorter the day, the clearer the man,
neither absolved nor condemned, without the rust of frost,
in the dark glade the gesture
like lightning reveals rocks:
folios, engravings of night,
but there is more to survive,
memory purges the life
from glacier to city,
illusions oppose the seed of an apple
every night,
in every room,
when one leaps from the highest cliff
and never becomes present tense

devoted walls stood there,
no one had a sword,
the hay bundled
into a bouquet meant more
than funereal chrysanthemums,
fog rose and fell,
could any least syllable of loneliness
escape november's yard

autumn apocalypse

toward the silence of plains
of hard-frozen earth one beam bends,
the heavy light settles
slowly on the face
and between the bell and night
consonance, created unexpectedly,
bears away dreams: right here,
where are scorching winds, where the returning
warrior bows to the reign of time,
a hand has opened doors to twilight,
an eye shatters the view
into the loneliness of things, but there is no heart,
only pulses, premonitions, and a step
beyond the rose traced by frost
on burning windows

gloria mundi

to embrace the night while splintered stars
pierce into drying skin,
to question yourself and to hear more
than whispers from the choir of the city's care,
when the moon turns,
the passions grow through glass twilights
and an hour looks in the window:
without limits, without echoed sighs,
say there is in every reflection
only the beginning: of the face, of the reign of hope,
we say the lonely name
but no moisture remains in it,
only a glass, empty and light,
fingers touch liberated lines,
salut, gloria mundi,
light and empty is our vision

who arose in our bodies,
with birds on wires the light
lingers, one station,
but no one meets trains,
times parallel, lines of a poem,
every kilometer is only
a chord of night,
when fingers
run through frozen forests
where we sleep, dreaming ourselves

dream proserpina

here the dam of the dream
here the raised arms
here fingers touch
                    secret
doors of consciousness
the drowsy city
                like an old ship
thrown into emptiness
from the crest of a wave
you come nearer
but the tide
            is only autumn in reverse
leaves
float up
from yards
and I admire you
faded dream proserpina

the fall

I would go
where the tangle of fallen trees
creaks in the sun
as if by itself
immersed
under the lining of snow
I would find reflections
I would find
the eyes of one ray
I would fall
from one world
into another
as if by itself
to the sun

antipygmalion

it will be time but not eternity.
a stone tureen under the heart.
the eye that fed me.

days shorten. night will come,
indifferent to passions. the dream
of the demiurge will visit, ascetic.

already. were it not for the words
that trapped you in a block of silence,
I would have tried to escape.

like the broken syllable of day
like stones in the foundation of the sanctuary
like this winter for which is too low
the evening sky

so invisible is the heart in the pulse
so inscrutable is the voice of god
so is your hour

losing death

in the glade of burning paper
letters receive sight: the sky where birds
nestle does not end with the day,

swollen shadow between sails,
the feeling carries flotsam,
tired thoughts ever nearing
decalogue, ever longer you load
your thoughts into time,
thinking over your past
life: unsolved,
wind wrinkled by the edge of an iceberg,
and again you are the last
left for the flame and word

arrow

like a diphthong between the fingers
is the poppy seed, erupting lava
catches the gesture and absorbs
times,
        you say: more death,
more dotted lines in life,
and evening disintegrates at your touch,
the axle of solitude, axis *mundi,*
but you wake
                hearing the extension of scale
and listen: as if spaces rang
because an arrow shivers in the vault

écoutez

écoutez, whispers july,
the days of this month are accounted for
and there is one guard left to us,
in the hollow of the vowel—white horse,
rains receive the beaten grass,
the east glints, a blow above midnight,
we are driven till the reins draw blood
by the red word of dawn, the hand
cannot reach this flower,
écoutez, but we have no ear,
and again reaping in the dew the scythe is sharpened
and again the honey of earth flows over us

sand sphinx

hot rocks, through slippery shadow
the voice dives into august,
wind splashes in sails, the citations of day,
and I speak from the palm: sand pours,
building a bridge to the sun
on your shoulder,
                                        only in this hour
can one read the handwriting of summer

dawn breaks: across your forehead
is stretched the river of midnight,

what timeless one
will bend over us, what spacing
wind will burst
                    the glow,

sickle of eyebrows wanes:
here is a vision,
                    and there
only a view of day

resurrected for those who do not exist,
tomorrow another color
will also light your hair
and water will wait for waving,
but now who, while yet
there is no world,
while the letter of chaos turns in the sun
and wonder penetrates spaces,
who could testify
in you: silent:
who crosses you like
an unending unlit street,
I am, but not the gods'
is this solitude, this autumn

stairs of megara

the black stairs of megara,
one hears step-by-step, the trunks
of lindens moan, here—hardened lava,
a stone necklace slips through fingers,

here—other customs,
between lovers billowy ferns blow,
more signs of eternity, fewer
of warmth, over the sources of childhood
and the meridian of winter the hand passes,
and again you lacked one hour,
through scattered mist poured
the rains of an instant

alien home

in the shapes of night I see
your gaze, obscure as a waning moon,
from the sunset, from the rising continent,
your beauty summoned: a sphinx's hour,
and words hang over the ravine,
soft dampness, death keeps getting tangled
in the uncombed hair, an answer
keeps coming in a mad lava like snow,
between the seductive shores
a ship with lowered sails is saved,
white fins of a swordfish,
shadows of fir trees, an alien home so near,
while I live in you, between your shut eyelashes,
an inspired blind man, a dreamer,
I have no home, only brackets of love
in the desperate silence of dictionaries

translated by Lionginas Pažūsis and H. L. Hix

morning in the land of visions,
lit by voices the stucco
of suburbs crumbles, poverty
befalls only those who cry,
beneath the ties—night,
and the train speeds, has faith
in continuance, uninhabited spaces
besieged by silence, but someone lived there once,
thousands of years ago, in the moment of solitude,
voices resound over empty territory:
you become king, and the diadem
of the moon pales, the bonfire
is fulfilled in wrinkles of ash: you wait
on the platforms of cities
by the flickering red eye of sidewalks

to the other side of blood
our rafts travel,
other words
salve our wounds, and others',
in one year of joy
corn gathered to granaries,
the lonely child among us
in revealed stubble

the one who stands

the head swims
under heavy cornices of roofs
years near
wearing faces of strangers

names and herbs
traces left
on the detritic leviathan

imponderable street
in the moon's dusty crater
the key to the intersection
where you stand tonight

who will punish you when you return from the land
of sins, I see, like a barge loaded
with ore the poem suffocates on the verge of night,
yes, fragile consonants break
under the weight of your life, but increasingly weightless
becomes the ur-syllable, the naked balance
of equation crosses days along rails on which
without slowing down trains disappear
into you, yes, it is the last station, where shadows
roam the platforms, looking for their idea,
for their reflection, for their soul,
but when I lean on the guillotine,
on the table over which the euphonic dream rows,
I fear the heart: in silence, in the canorous
tunnels of consciousness, traces end,
reserves end, on hands and knees
dampness lies down as if I lay down in morning
in the dampness of a rich field
and ursa major moved away
leaving me to the will of inspiration

sub specie aeternitatis

let it be only a light
breath of wind, having slid down
the throat an uncowed vowel
and a drop of wine spreading along
the edge of the glass, sustaining as memory,
here the evening in front of us,
here the glass, autumn rain,
here we ourselves, bent over the table,
in the endless fairy tale, silent

the accent of time is over us
grammar of silence in us
your angel and mine

you leave already (by the voiceless letter
one more door is locked)

behind the burning pleats of a continent
a child hides: laughter, barely suppressed,
barely guessed states
of a king, two-faced,
one can hide or give oneself up,

ever closer eyes (under lenten
garments) the spring,
flowing out in four directions,

the masks enjoy themselves, a laugh,
a laugh of dry wind (breast
dried by herbs), go

when your warmth
spreads
over holms and rocks
of the riverbed, I rise,
keeping in my palm
the instant of death,
ruddy leaf
rocking
at the top of memory,
and the icy gust
shows me
the way to you:
in the distance where I find
neither the reflection nor the voice
a darkness exhales you

ragged wing, diverting the current
of water, who will remember worn-out names,
the one who slipped, who is falling soundlessly,
bloody feathers that line the nest
of the griffin: you'll never confess
being weightless, never
throw down the body as a sacrifice:
only feathers, servants of the mind,
only the sweep of time, rinsed mouth
unsated by the morsel of loneliness:
like a syllable it makes a circle
and petrifies again in the death point
unreachable

while the day divides you stay
in the glare off the cornice, the echo
of corridors snatches the candle
from hands, and clay already burns,
let it be the middle, open hour,
but there is no time between dots,
a dotted line, a straight line, locked
fingers, let time be
in this drought when clouds burst
while smoke passes over the leaf,
forbidden territory becomes clear,
no one answers: silence in the palate,
doors on creaking hinges

evening tracks

candles melt
leaving luminous fog on the face

every year repeats
the mass for our dead image

every year the snow
over disintegrating dunes is whiter

winter nights grow longer
than our glow

every year

vox

the edge of the earth is lit by passion:
grass plots rot, in the depth of poison
the ur-syllable revolves,

beauty has not yet been spoken,
the demon of the pole still wears
time's mantle: overwhelmed by blood
you are recurrent

water

I was infinite water
that washed the beauty
of your tautness, but I was not in you
as is a baby in the womb,
I did not grow with you,
I avoided the crying void
you called the heart of eternity,
I withered there
where you stopped time, I was infinite,
and the limit was above me

translated by Mėta Žukaitė and H. L. Hix

necklace

of gray crumbs of day,
of leaning words and a city's accent,
this chain is on a neck

farther and farther away golden nets stretch
to margins of rain where are only dotted lines,
fragmented stories of consciousness,

but the flame grows clearer, and sands
like linden blossoms blast
exotic forms of hell: on the cape

of stone the runes of place-names glitter,
someone was here before spring died,
someone still bears stigmata in the look, harsh

as a cut word, though who
will say on whom the wound was inflicted
when fates were but the possibilities of the storm

when you could turn over images
and see the same, shallow identity,
everything is there under the water of being,

but unfortunately perfection sees farther,
surface is numb, though never
will the breast look more beautiful

by which a cold sign—the amulet of defense
crawls like heaven's snake up

the fog of castle roses

I

these places are more important, where rains intersect
and castle roses rise higher,
spinning us into the gust of time,

already we forget desolate lives
drowned in the eye sockets of dukes,
the victors in battle, stateless and free,

soon the shield of vritra melts,
things you believed in for centuries disrobe,
but the rushing rivers of flood season are more real,

o lord, only shed skins, but in prickly neglect
all colors are waved in, slow ornaments,
the remnants of heraldic belts,

it is our cloak fluttering
in the torn intersections of streets
where we shed the skin of the labyrinth

and the weather vane points to a temporal home,
what canvas could warm
the walls around a crumbling city

II

one word, piercing harmony,
and one body, turned into an hour,
still dance in slow flame, forgotten,

the eyes of a gorgon, the heart of an angel,
one hearing the call turns to us,
but the call comes from beyond,

without joy, as if guilty
the white smoke soaks into cloth,
we smell of eternal winter

III

longer and longer the bird incubates her eggs
on the precipice, numb, turned toward the glow
of the forest's edge, her narrow wing like pleats

of singed cloth covers us, clasps the sand
of the roadbed, the fog of castle roses,
but cracked space—no longer the lord's throne,

the empty dish is filled by winter angels,
only an invisible toast to the children of vilnius,
strange time, the guards loom

in the light of night pyramids,
a hungry dog, licking light, barks once
and into the dark mouth the universe vanishes

which key will absolve you of time?
beyond the heart's brief flare-up
lies a cleaving darkness, a world
burgeoning between two lips
of black earth, unanswered
by death, where life is accidental,
and love, impassable.

translated by Michael Theune

pilgrim

by strokes of hours,
by scorched leaves,
I ran around your house,
while autumn blazed in the clearings,
I leafed through book after book
looking for the bottom, but only mold
slid across my fingers, I spent nights
in an erotic dream, an enchanted circle,
everywhere, where there was warmth,
having lost fear and my erect
carriage, I fell down
hunched into the web
of my own shadows, I rose
as if from the grave, but hot autumn
flared in the eyes of insomnia:
I was together with the dead and the quick,
I was transparent, icy
stained glass, where drops of rain
probed deeper and deeper, where I gnawed
my chains, hands, lips,
having inherited age without hope,
I crossed the desert
as if along a narrow cornice
not holding on to you

pause

with a pause
your day also arrives:
it seems the shreds of evidence
are closed in their own time,
but behind the forest, behind the body,
petrified in an anesthetized voice,
trails in a train of the singed:
no longer will it be said
or written in blood on the forehead,
on the knuckles of the poet, you say: a perfect lie
is the longing of the lost tribe,
but perfect is your beast

peripheral vision

before the eye gets lost
the luster of rain settles
on surfaces, people,
pale pearls of suburbs,
cross silently into tomorrow
through *civitas mundi,*
still in their shells,
unhurt by the obscenity
of walls, graffiti on dusty windows,
even the one whose matte breasts
give respite to the glance, she too
is temporary, though before
you know that a shadow
of sense appears at the edge of night
only to slip away, leaving on your lips
the bitterness of reality

tabula rasa

who now will draw the clinking of crystal
from glass: from the heaven of the glade
where joy and ash join
by the silence of sanctuaries,
signboards over marketplaces, washed out
by rain, what do they testify,
innocent questions, surfacing
like water nymphs
on wrinkled rough drafts,
staying under the knowledge tree,
waiting for lightning, for clear insight,
one does not write impressions of hell,
tabula rasa, the glass grows dewy
exhaling the canto

enchanted country

drowsy apple trees, the wind still,
in this country without warmth
memory ripens slowly,
and even more slowly does a woman conceive,

in this country without an hour
to follow daylight home,
the glance goes wild, a rash breaks out,
in this country autumn never ends

translated by Mėta Žukaitė and H. L. Hix

under the cupola of snow

under the cupola of snow
memory spreading
                                        wider
you live without years:
from the pupil, from the burning amphora,
wine is poured into your joints,
the walls of blind alleys,
restlessly white the facade
of a café, night
                                keeps falling:
shorter and shorter lines
straggle in just before dawn

atlantis

that's all I see: the splintered relic of autumn,
in a narrow slit of sight
the continent shows white, ready to vanish,
the sun slides slowly over black enamel,

when I raise a full glass, and the shadows
of the earth suddenly match: unexpected
equilibrium before falling from a four-dimensional
world into a two-dimensional leaf,

the moment when a dizzy hand
draws the outline of the ocean
and the water submits to the art of cartography,
while seagulls call harshly, crying in zenith

à votre santé

to those who under collapsing cultures
learn not to be, between a rock
and a rock, mary and magdalene,
between tao and dada,

but all that ends in me,
when the eye shrinks into the virgin lead,
without alloy of time

à votre santé, to vanished continents,
to gratuitous creations
of the imagination in empty halls
during the apotheosis of the feast, during the very

lifting of hearts

crystallography

I

sight strikes the mote,
language climbs down the cornice,
vowels of fog
and sharp consonants,

clear hours partitioning the night,
everyone—like an ice floe flushed out
by voices, but silver nets
catch them too,

the cloth is quartered
and numb fingers grope
for a loose thread,
farther and farther,

where only destination is left
but not death, where the cloth
of stars is too bright
for an open wound,

the square piazza taps
out steps all night,
ever clearer the winter,
ever higher the white chiton of noah

II

shadows shattered
into sharp flashes catch in cloth,
only the blade of frost
strips the aura: the target of the sky

the trajectory of language
stretches over the longest nights—
myth
of ourselves falling to earth

III

by lips of frost
I create your image:
in the hollow of vowels
air trembles,

limitless
blue january,
starless moonlit night
but feeling in the light

like burnished copper,
along the outline of the body
the clock's hand
stencils

the monogram of being

crusade

with a gust of the autumn feast
the moon hangs over empty clearings
white as if washed all november
in gutters of rain
the god of war is pale
lovers point to the one who will sacrifice
their child for the crusade
to the graveyards of palestine
the child still in the womb listening
to the father's radiating despair and whisper:
what white what white
no wind and birds not scattering
over heads reflecting on love
descend slowly into the field of silence
hidden carefully from an alien plow
the ancient capital of the kingdom: what white
but feet tingle on hard-frozen earth
and like a flame stretched between palms
a saracen soldier leaps in the moonlight

dialogue in a cellar

the river's mouth swells and floods cellars,
gravel, herbs smelling of iodine—
the bed of the sleeping traveler
wrapped in his sunny dream,

who cares about him, who cares about an amphora
recovered from the holds of a foundered ship
near dardanelles strait,
a closed form in itself, not taking root
in the squares of rooms and the frames
of pictures? there are many aesthetics,
says the professor, and the strangest one
is under care of powers
that abhor us,

I accept your challenge, replies the poet,
I am not handsome, my voice
is monotonous and colorless,
I am no troubadour
with a codpiece, a sword at my side,
but nevertheless I am loved,

other times, the traveler says, taking leave,
we descend deep into underground vaults,
we write on damp walls words
we don't want to see
let's drink again and godspeed

north wind

I

no answer over the parting of your hair
the drop of blessing rolls deep in oil
blind rays intersect as long as the surface
glimmers you can guess the shore

no answer nobody asks
clarity is the scourge of god
a shower lashing aftermath of glass

what am I I ask today
on the slope drifted by the north wind
for the first time before the nuptials

with my dark side the chimera of childhood
her presents—foundered ships
coral words and dreams of the dead
I accept everything because the era ends

II

when my bony body tatters
the cloak of silence when my kidneys deliver
a sparkling pearl I am unlocked with a knife

and one more life holds the key
when the tramontane turns I lose everything
sand burns my mouth washes away visions
I become what I was not in the womb

embodiment of a dream that lost the body
perfect emancipated shape a conch
whistling in the wind

III

you strew crumbs in the sun
and the trace of birds dissipates in the fainting air
I want to catch up with those who fall down
into the rain who descend into the funnel

the lightning pulsing on the breast
and the dead heart call to each other
and renew the feast of the resurrection

every spring when the voice breaks down
I look for you in the lagoons knowing
only the direction of wind crossing obliquely
spray of the sea not asking anything

section 2 translated by Antanas Danielius and H. L. Hix

two thousand years

surrounded by woods a burning city:
open gates through which
for two thousand years gray legions pass
every time I returned carrying you
every time spears of jealousy
would pierce the prey: the young kshatriya warrior
with no right to eternal life

and indeed I would die before dawn
on the day of the funeral you would disappear
or change your voice: you would turn into martha
or mary or the pregnant suburban queen
only my ashes fertilizing the roots of your hair
tell of our bond

will the end of the world also meet us this way
two hands of the clock testifying against each other
and stopping nowhere the city of ash
and the delicate grass of the wood waiting for morning
I liked to count years but always
I started with death: thus begin
all the stories open gates through which
for two thousand years gray legions pass

translated by Mėta Žukaitė and H. L. Hix

the one who laughed at the dead

the one who laughed at the dead
dwelt among us so we could reach each other
or drip slowly—secretly alone—into thickets of books,
out of night's shroud, someone cooed a farewell,
in the grass snake's eyes summer's horizon ripped
and someone's hands gave out the days
but there were few who wanted them,

the one who laughed at the dead
was one of us though we couldn't identify him
or finger him for the high court's death sentence,
there were no secret renunciations, we believed
in belief and lived off the interest, waiting for the rain
to cover up our misguided paths so they would not return
those things we dreamed with open eyes,

the one who laughed at the dead
was our time, we drank,
two-handed, from the brimful amphora
to dizziness, to madness, to vomiting,
never seeing at the bottom
the eyes
of the one who laughed

translated by Michael Theune

the heian court

redness of roofs, a slow sight
still draws the last curve,
courtiers of the heian epoch
whisper among themselves, commenting
on the blossoming cherry branch, by hints,
by half-hieroglyphs, they meet
the absolute, and it accords
with the maxims of the wise,

regular features of the preacher
gladden the heart, as if one heard
the rustling on this side of the shoal,
we welcome the man coming toward us,
we flow into the play
of the capital, and it blooms,

to the harmony of the autocratic night
the silent emperor kneels,
we swear fealty waiting for our turn,
and it deceives

front

before the eye, where rage lines
flow together, there is nothing
time can explain,

at intervals, on splinters
of a breaking god, the sky clears,
the drunken sailor, steering the solitude
between scylla and charybdis, puts his head
here, on our hands, dying,
with a manichaean smile, as the darkness
of the epoch of genies falls: a bell covers

specks of dust but they do not pray,
while a tarpaulin-tight wind smooths the wrinkles,
whatever happens: a star, the bloody eye
of a bull or fish, we have no proof,

but the wind points toward the sail,
and the sail toward us, white goddess
of innocence and capitulation

civitas lunae

I

you thought you had guessed the name,
but the creek still runs free,
immersed hands feel the warts
of roots, the water stirs
more and more, every morning it is harder
to wake up: the faded landscape of dream
is incomparable, perhaps
civitas soli, but the city of the moon
would work better, in white shadows
and rounded roofs, changing shapes
but with the hovering singular soul
of its citizens,
what arrow will penetrate the doubt
of the intersection? you withdraw from the continent,
where flows win and ebbs
betray, astrological illnesses
haunt you, scorpio, pisces,
and libra watch you with pity

every word of prophecy
could be turned over and read through
or turned into number, so ancient
hebrew science teaches, but you take
from this home ridiculous old tools
hoping to deceive, while a moth
circles the candle, and again
the discharge of memory, again the rag

of the dream, a scarred crater of solitude,
as if you had been nowhere, as if no one
had gone anywhere

II

wider than the delta of spring
things spread: dates crossed out,
linguistic mechanisms broken,
along one side of the street
signs line up, people
here are silent, saving sight,

don't look for your reflection here,
thought is reflected by night, and a day
soaks up pain, an alien feeling
crumbles a body and weights a word,
but there is no city where the gates
do not open into solitude,

and the bell—into the labyrinth of the heart,
black ash falls into our words,
only the hand raised against yourself
sees a beast in a burned-out portico,
defeated force—only the gesture of kings
in the melting blue of a mirror

III

corners touched by shadow, the open moon,
only a worn-away crown protects

your face, only a lantern in the mind
rows over the land of the answer,
the rains with broken pediments,
received into pits, into smooth months,
without piercing arrows, without
the hangover of the word, but days left undrunk
pursue you: how much freedom in the blood
of a runaway, in apartment-hives of wild bees,
you entered by mistake, over the threshold
of consciousness, listening only to the hum,
erroneous the square of a room
and your circle, at intervals things
discover hands and light up,
but columns of water fall
when you touch a time not your own
and white cliffs like the teeth of pontos
bite the city: the geometry of wind
is too hard for you, poet

IV

I wish you the courage of an inquiring god,
the current of fresh water
laves the maps of palms,
fraying the outline (twitching
eyelid): too high a pressure
for the small mechanism of a clock,

too cramped a continent,
one river and one life:
crippled the crowns

of fir groves: only the wreaths
above the abyss of gravesites: fir branches,
spilling from a child's hand

apportion for yourselves
these days, phases of the moon,
because the eclipse of thought is near,
when words like scattered stars
will fall from darkness to darkness

and light-years in a clock spring,
and light under the earth:
letters, epitaphs, barometers:
between two underworlds,

and the geography of decline:
cities are being burned out,
only their coordinates left (suburbs
flourishing on trades of night)

V

a white branch, the sharp landscape of hedges,
the day is right here, you choose the street
raised from an icy dream,
burnished asphalt, hollow arches
and wind is favonian
into the infinite space of the raincoat,

but there is no need to hurry, time
is not yours, loitering below churches,
there are times, there is the baroque of night,

there is the renaissance of solitude,
but all this—later, when we drink
wine, mourning the broken glass of time,
only the key, evidence and weapon
in homeless hands, let it be so,

timeless being,
every step is full of silence,
so one names death, angel
and bird that crosses
the map of the city obliquely,
but turn around: red dye,
the heaviness of light
is being torn like the pilgrim's blossom

godspeed

you are descending swinging stairs
to bid godspeed to the sea,
godspeed, the salty lips of evening say,
and amber melts in the tongues of foam,

yes, emptiness strikes just then,
when the wine runs out, the salt settles
on roots and rolling sand starts
to desiccate rocks: at high noon,
when the hourglass is turned over, it strikes,

but the one who passes this,
like the youth who passes through the kingdom of death
to become a man, knows: it does not coincide
with the soul, as the mirage confirms

■ □ ■ □ ■

A NOTE ABOUT THE AUTHOR

EUGENIJUS ALIŠANKA WAS BORN IN 1960 AND IS CONSIDERED one of Lithuania's leading poets. His work includes articles on poetry and culture. *City of Ash* is his second collection of poetry; his first, *Equinox,* won the Zigmas Gėlė prize, given annually to the best debut book of Lithuanian poetry.

■ □ ■ □ ■

WRITINGS FROM AN UNBOUND EUROPE

Tsing
Words Are Something Else
DAVID ALBAHARI

City of Ash
EUGENIJUS ALIŠANKA

Skinswaps
ANDREJ BLATNIK

My Family's Role in the World Revolution and Other Prose
BORA ĆOSIĆ

Peltse and Pentameron
VOLODYMYR DIBROVA

The Victory
HENRYK GRYNBERG

The Tango Player
CHRISTOPH HEIN

A Bohemian Youth
JOSEF HIRŠAL

Mocking Desire
DRAGO JANČAR

Balkan Blues: Writing out of Yugoslavia
JOANNA LABON, ED.

The Loss
VLADIMIR MAKANIN

Compulsory Happiness
NORMAN MANEA

Zenobia
GELLU NAUM

Border State
TÕNU ÕNNEPALU

Rudolf
MARIAN PANKOWSKI

The Houses of Belgrade
The Time of Miracles
BORISLAV PEKIĆ

Merry-Making in Old Russia and Other Stories
The Soul of a Patriot
EVGENY POPOV

Estonian Short Stories
KAJAR PRUUL AND DARLENE REDDAWAY, EDS.

Death and the Dervish
The Fortress
MEŠA SELIMOVIĆ

Materada
FULVIO TOMIZZA

Fording the Stream of Consciousness
In the Jaws of Life and Other Stories
DUBRAVKA UGREŠIĆ

Angel Riding a Beast
LILIANA URSU

Shamara and Other Stories
SVETLANA VASILENKO

Ballad of Descent
MARTIN VOPENKA

The Silk, the Shears and *Marina; or, About Biography*
IRENA VRKLJAN

Time Gifts
ZORAN ŽIVKOVIĆ